Contents

Chapter 1   Elements and atomic structure   4

Chapter 2   The periodic table, calcium and the
            alkaline earth metals   6
            Elements of group 2   8
            More elements of group 2   10

Chapter 3   Trends in group 2   12
            Reactions with water in group 2   14
            Reasons to be reactive   16
            The isolation of the alkaline
                earth metals   18

Chapter 4   Beryllium   20
            Uses of beryllium   22

Chapter 5   Magnesium   24
            Uses of magnesium   26
            Magnesium compounds   28
            Magnesium and life   30

Chapter 6   Calcium   32
            Calcium carbonate   34
            Limestone and limewater   36
            Calcium, hardwater and health   38
            Bones   40
            Calcium oxide   42
            More calcium compounds   44

Chapter 7   Strontium   46
            Radioactive strontium   48

Chapter 8   Barium   50
            Barium compounds   52

Chapter 9   Radium   54
            Uses of radium   56

Find out more about the alkaline earth metals   58

Glossary   61

Timeline   63

Further reading and useful websites   63

Index   64

Words appearing in bold, **like this**, are explained in the Glossary

KT-117-256

CHAPTER 1

Elements and atomic structure

We are surrounded by different substances. All around us are metals, plastics, water and lots of other solids and liquids. There are gases in the air too, although you cannot see them. There are also many other gases. Amazingly, over 19 million different substances have been discovered, named, and catalogued. Around 4000 substances are added to the list each day, yet all of these substances are made from just a few simple building blocks called **elements**.

Elements and compounds

An element is a substance that cannot be broken down into simpler substances using chemical **reactions**. There are 92 naturally occurring elements and a few artificial ones. About three-quarters of the elements are metals, such as magnesium and calcium, and the rest are non-metals, such as oxygen and carbon. **Compounds** are made when elements join together in a chemical reaction. For example, magnesium and oxygen react together to make magnesium oxide, and carbon and oxygen react together to make carbon dioxide. This means that most of the millions of different materials in the world are compounds made up of two or more elements chemically joined together.

Atoms, protons, neutrons and electrons

Every substance is made up of tiny particles called **atoms**. Each element contains just one type of atom, but compounds are made from two or more types of atom joined together. Atoms are far too small to see, even with a light microscope. Radium atoms are the largest in group 2. If you could line up them up side by side along a 15 cm ruler, you would need 600 million of them!

Everything you can see here, even the coral (and fish) is made from the millions of substances in the world. Most of these substances, including the water, will be compounds.

Calcium

and the Alkaline Earth Metals

THE PERIODIC TABLE

Nigel Saunders

Heinemann

501 276 120

501276120

www.heinemann.co.uk/library

Visit our website to find out more information about Heinemann Library books.

To order:

☎ Phone 44 (0) 1865 888066

▤ Send a fax to 44 (0) 1865 314091

▢ Visit the Heinemann Bookshop at www.heinemann.co.uk/library to browse our catalogue and order online.

First published in Great Britain by Heinemann Library, Halley Court, Jordan Hill, Oxford OX2 8EJ, part of Harcourt Education. Heinemann is a registered trademark of Harcourt Education Ltd.

© Harcourt Education Ltd 2003
First published in paperback in 2004
The moral right of the proprietor has been asserted.

All rights reserved. No part of this publication may be reproduced, stored in a retrieval system, or transmitted in any form or by any means, electronic, mechanical, photocopying, recording, or otherwise, without either the prior written permission of the publishers or a licence permitting restricted copying in the United Kingdom issued by the Copyright Licensing Agency Ltd, 90 Tottenham Court Road, London W1T 4LP (www.cla.co.uk).

Editorial: Sarah Eason and Kathy Peltan
Design: David Poole and
     Tinstar Design Limited (www.tinstar.co.uk)
Illustrations: Geoff Ward and Paul Fellows
Picture Research: Rosie Garai
Production: Viv Hichens

Originated by Blenheim Colour Ltd
Printed and bound in Hong Kong and China by
     South China

ISBN 0 431 16981 0 (hardback)
07 06 05 04 03
10 9 8 7 6 5 4 3 2 1

ISBN 0 431 16988 8 (paperback)
08 07 06 05 04
10 9 8 7 6 5 4 3 2 1

British Library Cataloguing in Publication Data
Saunders, Nigel
     Calcium and the alkaline earth metals. –
     (The Periodic Table)
     546.3'9

A full catalogue record for this book is available from the British Library.

Acknowledgements
The publishers would like to thank the following for permission to reproduce photographs:

Corbis pp**10** (Jeffrey L Rotman), **19** (Archivo Iconografico), **23** (George Hall), **27**, **28** (Paul A Souders), **32** (Lester V Bergman), **35**, **47** (Yang Liu), **51** (Michael Nicholson); Ecoscene p**45**; Getty Images pp**8**, **39** (Amy Neunsinger); Hulton Archive p**54**; Oxford Scientific Films p**34** (T C Middleton); Peter Morris p**38**; Science Photo Library pp**13**, **57** (David Taylor), **15** top (Andrew Lambert), **20** (Roberto de Gulielmo), **24** (George Bernard), **30** (Dr Tim Evans), **37** top (Adam Hart Davis), **37** bottom (Jerry Schad), **41** (Biophoto Associates), **46** (Martin Land), **50** (E R Degginger), **53**, **55** (J C Revy); Trevor Clifford pp**29**, **33**; Trip pp**15** bottom (Andrew Lambert), **40** (H Rogers), **42** (Andrew Lambert), **44** (J Wender); Zefa p**4** (G Bell).

Cover photograph of chalk, reproduced with permission of Photodisc.

The author would like to thank Angela, Kathryn, David and Jean for all their help and support.

The publishers would like to thank Alexandra Clayton for her assistance in the preparation of this book.

Every effort has been made to contact copyright holders of any material reproduced in this book. Any omissions will be rectified in subsequent printings if notice is given to the publishers.

Disclaimer
All the Internet addresses (URLs) given in this book were valid at the time of going to press. However, due to the dynamic nature of the Internet, some addresses may have changed, or sites may have ceased to exist since publication. While the author and publishers regret any inconvenience this may cause readers, no responsibility for any such changes can be accepted by either the author or the publishers.

Atoms themselves are made up of even smaller particles called **protons**, **neutrons** and **electrons**. The protons and neutrons are found at the centre of each atom in a **nucleus**. The electrons are arranged in different shells around the nucleus. Most of an atom is actually empty space – if an atom were blown up to the same size as an Olympic running track, its nucleus would be about the size of a pea!
The number of the electrons in an atom and the way they are arranged in the shells determines the ways in which the element can react.

Elements and groups

Different elements react with other substances in different ways. When chemists first began to study chemical reactions this made it difficult for them to make sense of the reactions they observed. A Russian chemist called Dimitri Mendeleev was the most successful of these. In 1869, he put each element into one of eight **groups** in a table. Each group contained elements with similar chemical properties to each other. This made it much easier for chemists to work out what to expect when they made elements react with each other. Mendeleev's table was so successful that the modern **periodic table** is based closely on it.

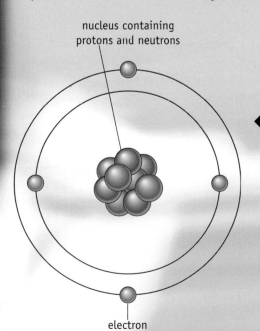

nucleus containing
protons and neutrons

electron

A model of an atom of beryllium. Every element has a different number of protons (atomic number). Each beryllium atom contains four protons and five neutrons. Its four electrons are arranged in two shells around the nucleus.

CHAPTER 2

The periodic table, calcium and the alkaline earth metals

The modern **periodic table**, shown here, is based closely on Mendeleev's table. Each row in the table is called a **period**, and the **elements** in a period are arranged in order of increasing **atomic number** (number of **protons** in the **nucleus**). Each column in the table is called a **group**. Within each group, the elements have similar chemical properties to each other. For example, all the elements in group 2 are very reactive metals, and all the elements in group 0 are very unreactive gases. The elements in each group also have the same number of **electrons** in their outer shell. The elements in group 2 all have two electrons in their outer shells. It is called the periodic table because these different chemical properties occur again regularly or periodically.

As you go down each group, the chemical properties of the elements change gradually. For example, the elements in group 2 become more reactive as you go down the group. Beryllium at the top does not react with water, calcium in the middle reacts quickly with water and barium near the bottom reacts very vigorously with water.

Calcium and the alkaline earth metals

In this book, you are going to find out all about calcium and the other **alkaline** earth metals in group 2, and many of their uses.

▼ *This is the periodic table of the elements. All the elements in group 2 are metals. They are beryllium, magnesium, calcium, strontium, barium and radium.*

Key

☐ metals

☐ metalloids

☐ non-metals

	group 3	group 4	group 5	group 6	group 7	group 0	
						⁴ **He** helium ₂	period 1
	¹¹ **B** boron ₅	¹² **C** carbon ₆	¹⁴ **N** nitrogen ₇	¹⁶ **O** oxygen ₈	¹⁹ **F** fluorine ₉	²⁰ **Ne** neon ₁₀	period 2
	²⁷ **Al** aluminium ₁₃	²⁸ **Si** silicon ₁₄	³¹ **P** phosphorus ₁₅	³² **S** sulphur ₁₆	³⁵ **Cl** chlorine ₁₇	⁴⁰ **Ar** argon ₁₈	period 3
⁵⁹ **Ni** nickel ₂₈ / ⁶⁴ **Cu** copper ₂₉ / ⁶⁵ **Zn** zinc ₃₀	⁷⁰ **Ga** gallium ₃₁	⁷³ **Ge** germanium ₃₂	⁷⁵ **As** arsenic ₃₃	⁷⁹ **Se** selenium ₃₄	⁸⁰ **Br** bromine ₃₅	⁸⁴ **Kr** krypton ₃₆	period 4
¹⁰⁶ **Pd** palladium ₄₆ / ¹⁰⁸ **Ag** silver ₄₇ / ¹¹² **Cd** cadmium ₄₈	¹¹⁵ **In** indium ₄₉	¹¹⁹ **Sn** tin ₅₀	¹²² **Sb** antimony ₅₁	¹²⁸ **Te** tellurium ₅₂	¹²⁷ **I** iodine ₅₃	¹³¹ **Xe** xenon ₅₄	period 5
¹⁹⁵ **Pt** platinum ₇₈ / ¹⁹⁷ **Au** gold ₇₉ / ²⁰¹ **Hg** mercury ₈₀	²⁰⁴ **Tl** thallium ₈₁	²⁰⁷ **Pb** lead ₈₂	²⁰⁹ **Bi** bismuth ₈₃	²⁰⁹ **Po** polonium ₈₄	²¹⁰ **At** astatine ₈₅	²²² **Rn** radon ₈₆	period 6
²⁸¹ **Ds** darmstadtium ₁₁₀ / ²⁸⁰ **Rg** roentgenium ₁₁₁ / ²⁸⁵ **Uub** ununbium ₁₁₂		²⁸⁹ **Uuq** ununquadium ₁₁₄		²⁹² **Uuh** ununhexium ₁₁₆			period 7

¹⁵⁹ **Tb** terbium ₆₅	¹⁶³ **Dy** dysprosium ₆₆	¹⁶⁵ **Ho** holmium ₆₇	¹⁶⁷ **Er** erbium ₆₈	¹⁶⁹ **Tm** thulium ₆₉	¹⁷³ **Yb** ytterbium ₇₀	¹⁷⁵ **Lu** lutetium ₇₁
²⁴⁷ **Bk** berkelium ₉₇	²⁵¹ **Cf** californium ₉₈	²⁵² **Es** einsteinium ₉₉	²⁵⁷ **Fm** fermium ₁₀₀	²⁵⁸ **Md** mendelevium ₁₀₁	²⁵⁹ **No** nobelium ₁₀₂	²⁶² **Lr** lawrencium ₁₀₃

f block

Elements of group 2

There are six **elements** in group 2: beryllium, magnesium, calcium, strontium, barium and radium. They are fairly soft, silvery-white metals, which are all solids at room temperature. With the exception of beryllium, they all react with water to make **alkaline** solutions. This is why they are often called the alkaline earth metals.

9		**beryllium**
Be		symbol: Be • atomic number: 4 • metal
beryllium		
4		

Where is it found? The name beryllium comes from beryl, one of the **minerals** in which it is found. Emeralds are precious stones made from beryl that contains a small amount of a metal called chromium. Chromium gives emeralds their green colour.

What is it like? Beryllium is the least reactive alkaline earth metal. A very thin layer of beryllium oxide covers its surface and gives it a grey colour. This layer protects the metal beneath from reacting with oxygen in the air, or with water.

What are its main uses? Beryllium itself is **brittle**, but when mixed with other metals it produces **alloys** that are light and strong. These alloys are used in aircraft and spacecraft. Once chemists discovered beryllium, they quickly discovered that its compounds have a sweet taste. However, beryllium compounds are very poisonous.

Emeralds contain beryl, which is a **compound** called beryllium aluminium silicate. Emeralds are green because they also contain tiny amounts of chromium and vanadium.

<table>
<tr><td>24
Mg
magnesium
12</td><td>**magnesium**
symbol: Mg • atomic number: 12 • metal</td></tr>
</table>

Where is it found? Magnesium is named after an area of Greece called Magnesia, in which minerals containing magnesium are mined.

What is it like? Magnesium is more reactive than beryllium, and it burns vigorously with a dazzling white flame when heated in air.

What are its main uses? Magnesium is used in flares, fireworks and incendiary bombs. Magnesium alloys are used in missiles, aircraft and drinks cans. Magnesium oxide has a very high melting point and is used to make bricks for furnace linings. Many magnesium compounds are harmful, and may irritate your eyes and throat. Others, such as magnesium hydroxide are safe to use in medicines. 'Milk of Magnesia', which is often used to cure an upset stomach, contains magnesium hydroxide powder mixed with water.

<table>
<tr><td>40
Ca
calcium
20</td><td>**calcium**
symbol: Ca • atomic number: 20 • metal</td></tr>
</table>

The name calcium comes from the Latin word for lime (calcium oxide).

Where is it found? Calcium is found in minerals such as limestone, chalk and marble, which are all forms of calcium carbonate.

What is it like? Calcium is more reactive than magnesium, and when heated in air, it burns with a red flame.

What are its main uses? Calcium is an important mineral in our diet – our bones and teeth contain a lot of it. Calcium oxide is used in cement and concrete, and calcium carbonate is used in iron and steel making. If you have ever broken a bone, you might have had a cast made from plaster of Paris, which is calcium sulphate.

More elements of group 2

88 **Sr** strontium 38	**strontium** *symbol: Sr • atomic number: 38 • metal*

Where is it found? Strontium is named after a town in Scotland called Strontian, where **minerals** containing strontium are mined.

What is it like? Strontium is more reactive than calcium and needs to be kept under oil to stop air or water reaching it. It is so reactive that powdered strontium bursts into bright red flames on its own in air!

What are its main uses? Strontium nitrate and strontium chlorate produce a bright crimson flame when burnt and are used in tracer bullets, fireworks and signal flares. Other strontium **compounds** are used in toothpastes and the glass for colour television tubes. **Isotopes** are atoms of an **element** that have different numbers of **neutrons**. There are four natural isotopes of strontium. There are also at least twelve artificial isotopes, which are **radioactive**. The most stable radioactive isotope is strontium-90, which was released in the middle of the last century when nuclear bombs were tested above ground.

▼ *Strontium provides the red coloured flame in flares like this.*

137 Ba barium 56	**barium**
	symbol: Ba • atomic number: 56 • metal

Where is it found? The main **ore** of barium is barite, which is barium sulphate. Barite is very dense, and barium is named after the Greek word for heavy.

What is it like? Barium is more reactive than strontium and also needs to be kept under oil to stop air and water reaching it. When it burns in air, barium produces a very attractive apple green flame.

What are its main uses? Barium itself has very few uses, and many barium compounds are poisonous. Barium nitrate is very commonly used in fireworks, and barium carbonate is used as rat poison! Doctors use barium sulphate when they want to examine intestines using X-rays because it shows up white on X-ray photographs. It is safe to use because it does not dissolve in water and so cannot be absorbed by our bodies.

226 Ra radium 88	**radium**
	symbol: Ra • atomic number: 88 • metal

What is it like? Radium is a very radioactive metal that glows in the dark. It is named after the Latin word for ray. Marie Curie first discovered radium in 1898, and managed to isolate it in 1911. At the time, very little was known about radiation. Many researchers, including Marie Curie herself, became ill as a result of their experiments.

What are its main uses? In the past, radium was widely used to treat cancer, and compounds such as radium chloride were used to make paints for watch dials and aircraft dials that glow in the dark. However, radium is very expensive and can cause **radiation** burns. As a result it now has little practical use in our everyday lives.

CHAPTER 3

Trends in group 2

The **alkaline** earth **elements** react with oxygen, dilute acid and water in similar ways. Some elements are more reactive than others, however, particularly those at the bottom of the group. Beryllium at the top of the group is the least reactive and radium at the bottom is the most reactive, although it is difficult to study its chemistry because it is both rare and **radioactive**. Gradual changes in properties like these are called trends.

Reactions with oxygen

All the alkaline earth metals react with oxygen to form metal oxides. For example, magnesium reacts with oxygen to produce magnesium oxide, MgO, and calcium reacts with oxygen to produce calcium oxide, CaO. A thin layer of metal oxide usually covers the surfaces of the alkaline earth metals. If the metal is cut or scratched, the layer is broken and you can see the silvery metal beneath. The exposed metal quickly reacts with oxygen in the air and forms the layer of metal oxide again. This **reaction** is very useful because the layer of metal oxide stops the metal beneath reacting with any more oxygen, unless it is powdered or heated.

Beryllium will only react with oxygen when it is powdered and heated. Magnesium will set on fire when heated and burns with an extremely bright white light. School teachers always advise their pupils to look away from the flame because intense light can damage their eyesight without any warning pain. Calcium is more reactive than magnesium, but its protective layer can make it difficult to set on fire. However, if calcium is freshly cut and heated, it explodes with sparks and a red flame!

Reactions with dilute acids

All the alkaline earth metals react with dilute acids to produce metal **salts** and hydrogen gas. Beryllium is unusual because it will also react with alkalis to produce complex beryllium salts and hydrogen. The other metals will only react with acids.

When the alkaline earth metals react with acids they make metal salts and hydrogen (H_2). The salt made depends upon the metal and acid used. For example, if magnesium reacts with hydrochloric acid (HCl) it makes magnesium chloride ($MgCl_2$). If magnesium reacts with sulphuric acid (H_2SO_4) it makes magnesium sulphate ($MgSO_4$).

magnesium + hydrochloric → magnesium + hydrogen
acid   chloride

magnesium + sulphuric → magnesium + hydrogen
acid   sulphate

Magnesium ribbon reacts very quickly with acids such as hydrochloric acid. Heat and lots of bubbles of hydrogen gas are produced in these reactions. These bubbles make the magnesium float on the surface of the acid. When magnesium reacts with hydrochloric acid, the salt produced is magnesium chloride. This dissolves quickly in the acid, causing the metal to disappear from sight. Depending upon the strength and temperature of the acid, small pieces of magnesium can vanish in a few seconds, and calcium reacts even more quickly!

◄ *Magnesium ribbon burning with a brilliant white light in oxygen to make magnesium oxide. If magnesium ribbon is burned in air, some magnesium nitride is also made, because the magnesium can react with nitrogen in the air.*

Reactions with water in group 2

Beryllium does not react with water or steam, even if it is heated very strongly. However, all the other **alkaline** earth metals react with water to produce metal hydroxides and hydrogen. For example, magnesium reacts with water to produce magnesium hydroxide, $Mg(OH)_2$, and calcium reacts with water to produce calcium hydroxide, $Ca(OH)_2$. These are white solids that do not dissolve particularly well in water, but do so enough to make the water alkaline.

When the alkaline earth metals react with water they make metal hydroxides and hydrogen. For example, the word equation for magnesium reacting with water is:

magnesium + water → magnesium hydroxide + hydrogen

Magnesium

People often expect magnesium to react violently with water because it burns so brightly in air. However, magnesium reacts very slowly with water, producing tiny bubbles of hydrogen over several days. Some of the magnesium hydroxide produced dissolves in the water, making it slightly alkaline. Although this reaction is a little disappointing, it is a different story if magnesium is heated in steam!

Magnesium burns with a blinding white light when it is heated in steam. The reaction makes a lot of hydrogen gas which, with care, can be set on fire. The flame keeps burning as long as there is enough magnesium left to react with the steam. If the amount of steam used is limited, magnesium oxide is made instead of magnesium hydroxide. If a lot of steam is used in the reaction, some of it reacts with the magnesium oxide to produce magnesium hydroxide, which is also produced when magnesium reacts with water.

▲ *Magnesium ribbon burning in steam to make magnesium oxide and hydrogen. If the water used to make the steam contains dissolved calcium and sodium salts, the flame can be coloured like this.*

Calcium, strontium and barium

Calcium is found below magnesium in the **periodic table.** It reacts with cold water far more quickly than magnesium and produces a lot of bubbles of hydrogen over just a few minutes. The water can get quite hot during the reaction, and becomes cloudy white. This is because only some of the calcium hydroxide produced dissolves in it. The rest forms a suspension (tiny bits of undissolved calcium hydroxide mixed with the water). Strontium reacts with water more quickly than magnesium and calcium. Barium, near the bottom of the group, reacts immediately with water and produces lots of large bubbles of gas very quickly.

Dangerous alkalis

Calcium hydroxide solution and other alkalis are irritants, and must be treated carefully. If spilt on your skin, they will feel soapy. This is because they react with the oils on your skin to make soapy chemicals. They can also cause skin burns, and are particularly dangerous if they get into your eyes. You must always wear eye protection in the laboratory when experimenting with them and take care not to get them on your skin.

◀ *Calcium reacting vigorously with water to make alkaline calcium hydroxide and bubbles of hydrogen gas.*

Reasons to be reactive

Electrons in an **atom** are arranged in shells around the **nucleus**. Chemists are usually interested in the shell furthest from the nucleus, called the outer shell. If this shell is filled completely with electrons, the atom will be unreactive. The noble gases, which include helium and neon, are very unreactive because their atoms have full outer shells of electrons. However, if the outer shell is not filled completely with electrons, the atom will react with other atoms to get a full outer shell. In a chemical **reaction** between a metal like magnesium, and a non-metal like chlorine, the atoms fill their outer shells by passing electrons from one to the other.

▼ *The atoms of each group 2 element get bigger as you go down the group. The two electrons in the outer shell get further from the nucleus. These are the colours of their flames.*

Be Mg Ca Sr Ba Ra

It's all about electrons!

Non-metals atoms often need just one, two or three more electrons to fill their outer shell. As a result, they get electrons from another atom to fill their outer shell. Metal atoms are just the opposite. They have unfilled outer shells, often containing just one, two or three electrons, and they can consequently give these electrons away to another atom. This leaves the shell beneath, which is full of electrons, as the new outer shell.

None of the atoms of the **group** 2 metals have full outer shells. Instead, they have just two electrons in their outer shells. When the metals react with non-metals, these electrons are transferred to the non-metal atoms. The more easily this happens, the more reactive the metal will be.

Losing electrons

Beryllium atoms are very small compared to the others in the group. The electrons in the outer shell are close to the nucleus of the atom, and are very strongly attracted to it. As a result, the electrons are difficult to lose and beryllium is fairly unreactive. As we move down the elements of group 2, the atoms get bigger and bigger. As a result, the two electrons in the outer shell are further and further away from the nucleus. They become less strongly attracted to the nucleus and so are lost more easily in reactions. This makes the **elements** further down the group more reactive. Radium is found at the bottom of the group. It has the largest atoms and so is the most reactive.

The reactivity series

If metals are listed in order of their reactivity, the list is called a reactivity series. It is possible to make a large reactivity series by studying the reactions of metals other than the **alkaline** earth metals. Chemists can work out how a metal should react by looking at its position in the reactivity series.

The reactivity series		
element	**group**	
potassium	1	most
sodium	1	reactive
lithium	1	
calcium	**2**	
magnesium	**2**	
aluminium	3	
zinc	transition metal	
iron	transition metal	
tin	4	
lead	4	
copper	transition metal	
silver	transition metal	
gold	transition metal	least
platinum	transition metal	reactive

The isolation of the alkaline earth metals

The **alkaline** earth metals were all discovered some years before they were isolated – discovering an **element** can involve a process quite different from isolating it. When chemists are certain that they have found a new element, they have discovered it. However, these chemists might not be the ones who manage to isolate it. Isolation involves separating the new element from other elements to make it into a pure sample. A long time may pass before chemists manage to do this. The alkaline earth metals were not isolated until electricity was discovered.

Twitching frogs and batteries

An Italian biologist called Luigi Galvani was interested in discovering how the bodies of animals function. He was in for a bit of a shock! In 1791 he carried out some experiments with dead frogs and observed that they started twitching whenever he tried to pin them to an iron frame using brass pins! By accident, Galvani had discovered that muscles twitch when electricity passes through them.

Galvani thought that the electricity came from the bodies of the dead frogs, but another Italian scientist called Alessandro Volta realised that it actually came from the two different metals. He was able to use this information to make the first battery. Volta announced his new invention in 1800, and chemists rushed to test it with all sorts of chemicals to see what would happen.

Electricity and electrolysis

Within months of Volta's invention of the battery, the English chemist William Nicholson discovered that electricity can be used to split water up into its two elements, hydrogen and oxygen. When electricity is used to split up or **decompose** a **compound** into its elements, it is called **electrolysis**.

In 1807 another English chemist, Sir Humphry Davy, used electrolysis to isolate potassium metal from molten potassium hydroxide. He was so excited by his discovery that he danced around his laboratory! Davy then set out to isolate other elements from their compounds using electrolysis. In 1808 he managed to isolate magnesium, calcium, strontium and barium. However, beryllium and radium were not isolated until some time later.

Beryllium

In 1828, the German chemist Friedrich Wöhler managed to isolate beryllium by heating beryllium chloride with potassium. Sir Humphry Davy had discovered how to isolate potassium using electrolysis 21 years earlier. So, although electrolysis was not used to isolate beryllium, it was needed to make the potassium that Wöhler used when he isolated beryllium.

Radium

Radium was discovered much later than the other alkaline earth metals, and was not isolated until 1911. Once again, the metal was isolated using electrolysis. Radium was not only discovered by the Polish-French chemist Marie Curie in 1898, but also isolated by her.

◀ A replica of one of Volta's batteries, which used discs made from two different metals such as zinc and copper, or zinc and silver. Each disc was separated by paper soaked in salty water or acid, and stacked in a glass tube. A pile of twenty or more pairs of metal discs could deliver quite a painful electric shock.

CHAPTER 4

Beryllium

Beryllium is a very hard, **brittle**, grey metal. A thin layer of beryllium oxide covers its surface, which protects the metal from reacting with water or steam, even when strongly heated. However, beryllium will react with oxygen if heated to about 600 °C. The original name for beryllium was glucinium, meaning sweet. It was so called because chemists discovered that beryllium **compounds** have a sweet taste. Unfortunately, they are also very poisonous and can cause skin rashes.

Dust containing beryllium and its compounds can cause a lung disease called berylliosis. The lungs of sufferers become swollen and inflamed and they find it difficult to breathe. We are unlikely to be exposed to beryllium in our everyday lives, but beryllium and beryllium compounds are important industrial hazards, and must be handled very carefully.

The discovery and isolation of beryllium

A French chemist called Louis Vauquelin discovered beryllium in 1798. He studied some crystals of beryl and emerald that were sent to him by René Haüy, a fellow Frenchman who believed that substances with identical crystals must also be chemically identical. Beryl and emerald crystals are very similar, and Vauquelin was able to show that they did contain the same chemical. He was also able to show that they contained a new **element**, beryllium. However, he was unable to isolate it. The French chemist Antoine-Alexandre-Brutus Bussy, and the German chemist Friedrich Wöhler, both isolated beryllium by heating mixtures of potassium and beryllium chloride in 1828.

Aquamarine is a precious stone ▶
containing beryl. It is this colour
because it contains small amounts
of iron. There is a myth that says
it is the mermaid's treasure and
that it keeps sailors safe at sea.

*The word equation for the **reaction** Bussy and Wöhler used is:*

beryllium + potassium $\xrightarrow{\text{heat}}$ beryllium + potassium
chloride   chloride

*The reaction happens because potassium is higher up in the reactivity series than beryllium. Consequently it is able to **displace** beryllium from beryllium chloride. The potassium chloride made in the reaction dissolves easily in water to leave solid beryllium behind.*

Extraction of beryllium

Beryllium is found in about 30 **minerals**, including beryl and the precious stones, emerald and aquamarine. Beryl is a compound called beryllium aluminium silicate, which contains beryllium, aluminium, silicon and oxygen. It is the most important industrial source of beryllium. About 280 tonnes of beryl is mined each year, two-thirds of it in the USA.

The extraction of beryllium from beryl happens in two stages. In the first stage beryl is heated strongly with a compound called sodium hexafluorosilicate to produce beryllium fluoride. In the second stage, the beryllium fluoride is mixed with magnesium and heated to around 900 °C. This reaction produces beryllium and magnesium fluoride.

The word equation for the second stage in beryllium extraction is:

beryllium + magnesium $\xrightarrow{\text{heat}}$ beryllium + magnesium
fluoride   fluoride

The reaction happens because magnesium is higher up in the reactivity series than beryllium, so it is able to displace beryllium from beryllium fluoride.

Uses of beryllium

Beryllium is more resistant to bending than steel, but it is less dense than aluminium. It also has a high melting point compared to other light metals. It can be mixed with other metals to make lots of different **alloys**, and it has some interesting properties that allow it to be used in nuclear reactors and X-ray machines.

Beryllium metal

Beryllium is used to make parts for aircraft and spacecraft which must be both light and strong. It is used in high-speed aircraft and satellites – the Space Shuttles contain window frames and supporting beams made from the metal. Beryllium conducts heat well and it has a high heat capacity. This means that it can absorb a lot of heat energy without becoming as hot as other metals. It is so efficient that it is used in the brakes of the Space Shuttle. These produce tremendous amounts of heat, as the shuttle is very heavy and touches down much faster than a normal aircraft.

Windows and moderators

Beryllium has some useful nuclear properties. It is not transparent to ordinary light, but does allow X-rays to pass through it easily. As a result, it is used in the windows of X-ray machines and **radiation** detectors.

The heart of a nuclear power station is its reactor core, where **atoms** of metals such as uranium break apart and release energy. When a high-speed **neutron** hits a uranium atom, the atom splits into two. When it does so, it releases some energy and three more neutrons. These neutrons then go on to split more uranium atoms. This is called a chain reaction, and it produces the heat energy in the reactor. The speed of the neutrons is very important in these chain reactions. Beryllium is used to slow down any neutrons travelling too fast to split the uranium atoms. Substances that can do this, like beryllium, are called moderators.

▲ *Lightweight beryllium alloys are used in engine components and in guidance and sensor systems of military helicopters.*

On your bike!

Copper is a very good conductor of electricity, but beryllium-copper alloys are much tougher. They are used to make electrical contacts in mobile phones and computers, and special tools that do not cause sparks when they are used. These are particularly useful in dusty factories where a stray spark could cause an explosion. Beryllium-aluminium alloys are lighter and stiffer than aluminium and are used in the manufacture of satellites, helicopters, golf clubs, bicycle frames and any object that requires a low weight.

Beryllium compounds

Beryllium chloride is used as a **catalyst** in the chemical industry to speed up reactions. Beryllium oxide is an insulator used in electrical circuits and car electronic ignition systems. It is also used in the armour for army tanks, and in microwave ovens and gyroscopes. Green crystals of beryllium aluminium silicate are cut to shape and sold as gemstones. They are, of course, known more commonly as emeralds.

CHAPTER 5

Magnesium

Magnesium is a soft, silvery-white metal. It has a low **density** (lower than that of beryllium), which makes pieces of magnesium feel light for their size. It is usually too weak to be used on its own, and is mixed with other **elements** to produce light but strong **alloys**. A thin layer of magnesium oxide covers its surface, which protects the metal from reacting with air or water unless it is heated strongly. However, magnesium reacts rapidly with acids even when cold. Molten magnesium must be protected from the oxygen in air by gases such as sulphur dioxide.

The discovery and isolation of magnesium

In 1755, a Scottish chemist called Joseph Black discovered magnesium while studying the reactions of magnesium and calcium **compounds**. Black studied magnesia, which we now know is magnesium oxide, and lime, which we now know is calcium oxide. At the time, chemists did not know which elements were in these compounds, but Black was able to show that substances made from magnesia were different from those made from lime. When he reacted magnesia with sulphuric acid, he made a **salt** that dissolved in water. A similar experiment using lime produced a **salt** that did not dissolve in water. From his experiments, Black knew that magnesia contained a different metal from the metal in lime, but he could not isolate it. Magnesium was not isolated until electricity was discovered.

In 1808, Sir Humphry Davy isolated magnesium by passing electricity through a mixture of molten magnesium oxide and mercury oxide. For his **electrolysis** experiments, Davy built the world's largest battery with 2000 pairs of metal discs!

▲ Joseph Black, 1728–99, whose experiments with magnesium and calcium compounds led him to discover magnesium, although he was unable to isolate it.

Extraction of magnesium

Magnesium is the eighth most abundant element in the Earth's crust and makes up about 2.5 per cent of it. **Minerals** such as dolomite and magnesite contain magnesium compounds, but magnesium is never found naturally as the free metal. Each cubic metre of seawater has over 1.3 kg of magnesium dissolved in it. As a result most magnesium is extracted from seawater rather than from minerals.

In the first stage of the extraction process, calcium oxide is added to seawater, which causes solid magnesium hydroxide to form. This is collected and reacted with hydrochloric acid to make magnesium chloride, $MgCl_2$.

The word equation for the production of magnesium chloride is:

magnesium + hydrochloric → magnesium + water
hydroxide   acid   chloride

In the second stage, the magnesium chloride is melted and electricity is passed through it. Magnesium is produced at the negative electrodes and floats to the top of the molten magnesium chloride. Chlorine gas is produced at the positive electrodes. It is collected and used to make more hydrochloric acid for the first stage.

negative electrode   molten magnesium chloride

positive electrode

◄ *The production of magnesium by electrolysis. The molten magnesium chloride contains electrically charged particles called **ions**. The magnesium ions are positively charged and are attracted to the negative electrode, where they become magnesium atoms.*

Uses of magnesium

Magnesium is quite high in the reactivity series, so it is able to displace less reactive **elements** from their **compounds**. This is very useful in metal production and rust prevention. Magnesium can be mixed with other metals to produce lightweight **alloys**.

Metal production

The final stage in producing uranium metal from its **ore** is called the Ames process. Uranium tetrafluoride is mixed with lots of powdered magnesium and heated in a special container. The **reaction** gives out so much heat that the temperature goes up to more than 1300 °C, which melts the magnesium fluoride slag and uranium is produced. The slag floats on top of the uranium and is removed when the container is cooled down again.

The word equation for the reaction in the Ames process is:

magnesium + uranium tetrafluoride → magnesium + uranium fluoride

The reaction happens because magnesium is higher up in the reactivity series than uranium, so it is able to displace uranium from uranium tetrafluoride.

Steel is iron that contains less than 2 per cent carbon, with other elements added to it to improve its properties. Some elements, such as sulphur, must be removed from the steel while it is being made. To do this, magnesium powder is blown into the molten steel. Magnesium is more reactive than iron and removes the sulphur from it, forming a magnesium sulphide slag. This floats on the molten steel and is scraped off.

Sacrificial protection

Iron and steel objects corrode and become rusty when they are exposed to oxygen and water. To stop them rusting, they are usually painted, oiled or coated in plastic.

However, this is not always easy to do, and paint can chip or flake off leaving the metal exposed. Another method to prevent rust, called sacrificial protection, is used for large ships, pipelines and oilrigs. A large bar of magnesium is bolted on to the object or connected to it with a cable. As magnesium is more reactive than iron, it corrodes instead of the steel. As long as the magnesium stays in contact with the steel, all the steel is protected. However, the magnesium is gradually eaten away and has to be replaced every so often. This process is still easier than trying to paint a large object in difficult places.

Magnesium alloys

Magnesium has a low **density** and as a result objects made from it are light for their size. Unfortunately, magnesium is relatively weak compared to other metals and is usually mixed with other metals to make alloys. Duralumin is a lightweight but strong alloy discovered early in the 20th century by Alfred Wilm. It is mostly aluminium, with about 4 per cent copper, between 0.5 per cent and 1.5 per cent magnesium, and some manganese. Duralumin is easily worked into shape, but becomes much harder and stronger when treated with heat. It is widely used in aircraft, spacecraft, cars and other machinery.

▲ *Most commercially produced magnesium metal is extracted from seawater. Magnesium alloys are lightweight and are extremely useful in the aerospace industry.*

Magnesium compounds

Magnesium reacts vigorously with oxygen when heated in air to produce a blinding white light. This **reaction** is used in distress flares, fireworks and in some types of flash photography. The magnesium oxide produced is one of several very useful magnesium **compounds**.

Magnesia bricks

The biggest single use for magnesium compounds is in refractory bricks. These are special bricks that are used to line the inside of blast furnaces, ovens and kilns. The best ones, called magnesia bricks, contain magnesium oxide. This has a very high melting point, 2852 °C, so it is very useful for making refractory bricks. Magnesite **ore** (magnesium carbonate) is heated strongly to make periclase (magnesium oxide), which is then made into bricks. Without these refractory bricks, blast furnaces would melt when being used!

▲ *Eight-inch thick steel blocks are re-heated to a nearly molten state. This furnace is lined with refractory bricks made from magnesium oxide to deal with the heat.*

Milk of Magnesia

Your stomach contains hydrochloric acid. This is needed to kill harmful bacteria that might be in your food, and it provides the acidic conditions needed to digest proteins. However, you can get indigestion if your stomach produces too much acid. Antacids are medicines that help to cure the indigestion by reacting with the extra acid. One antacid is called 'Milk of Magnesia'. It is a thick white suspension of magnesium hydroxide in water. When you swallow some, it reacts with some of the hydrochloric acid, which makes you feel better.

The word equation for the reaction of magnesium hydroxide with hydrochloric acid is:

$$\text{magnesium} + \text{hydrochloric} \rightarrow \text{magnesium} + \text{water}$$
$$\text{hydroxide} \quad\quad \text{acid} \quad\quad \text{chloride}$$

Magnesium hydroxide is also used as a flame retardant. These are chemicals that make it more difficult to set material or plastic on fire. When it is heated, magnesium hydroxide takes in heat energy and breaks down to release water vapour. This reaction helps to keep the plastic cool for longer in a fire.

Like a dose of Epsom Salt

Magnesium sulphate is often called Epsom Salt. It gets its name from the **mineral** water at Epsom in England, which naturally contains magnesium sulphate found in a mineral called epsomite. Commercial quantities of Epsom Salt are made by reacting magnesium carbonate with sulphuric acid. It has many uses, including cement and **fertilizer** manufacture, cosmetic lotions, bath salts, fireproofing and the 'snow' in films. Large doses of magnesium salts can cause diarrhoea, but used carefully Epsom Salt is a traditional laxative that can help if you are constipated.

Magnesium chloride

Magnesium chloride is drying agent. It is added to foods such as tinned vegetables to help keep them firm. It is also used to remove snow and ice from roads in the winter. When **salts** such as magnesium chloride are mixed with ice, they lower its melting point. Magnesium chloride melts ice right down to –15 °C, and does less damage to plants and concrete than other salts, such as sodium chloride. However, roads treated with it can become slippery if no snow falls because it absorbs moisture from the air.

◀ *Epsom Salt is used to reduce swelling and help bruises. It is also used in the dyeing of some textiles and in leather tanning.*

Magnesium and life

Cattle and sheep can develop a condition called 'grass tetany' or 'grass staggers' if they do not get enough magnesium in their diet. This makes it difficult for the animals to control their movements. They twitch and stagger about, and they can die in severe cases. Adding magnesium chloride to their food can prevent this illness. Magnesium is important to living things in a number of other ways.

Magnesium in the body

Magnesium is an important **mineral** in our diet because it plays a vital part in the chemistry of our cells. **Enzymes** are biological **catalysts** that are made from proteins, and many of them need 'co-factors' to work properly. Co-factors are metal ions – metal **atoms** that have lost **electrons** from their outer shells. Magnesium **ions** (Mg^{2+}) are co-factors for enzymes that control the release of energy by our cells. Without magnesium, our nerves and muscles would not work properly. This is why animals suffer from the 'staggers' if they do not get enough magnesium in their diet. Our recommended daily allowance for magnesium is 350 mg, but magnesium deficiency is rare because green vegetables contain a lot of it.

Magnesium ions play a vital part in keeping the DNA in our cells in its helical shape. ▶

Chlorophyll

Green plants can make their own food in a process called **photosynthesis**. This uses the energy from light to react carbon dioxide and water together, making glucose and oxygen.

The word equation for photosynthesis is:

$$\text{carbon dioxide} + \text{water} \xrightarrow{\text{light}} \text{glucose} + \text{oxygen}$$

Photosynthesis can happen in plant cells because they contain tiny objects called chloroplasts. Animal cells do not contain chloroplasts, so animals cannot make their own food. Chloroplasts contain a green protein called chlorophyll, which absorbs the light needed for photosynthesis. The world's plants make about 300 tonnes of chlorophyll per second, making it one of the most abundant proteins on Earth. At the heart of each chlorophyll **molecule** there is a magnesium **ion**.

The magnesium ion is vital for chlorophyll to work. If it is removed, the chlorophyll turns brown-green and cannot absorb light properly. This is unlikely to happen in a living plant, but it can happen when green vegetables are cooked.

Chlorophyll in cabbage

If you are unlucky, your dinner may contain limp brown-green cabbage! Green vegetables lose their colour if they are cooked too long because the chlorophyll gets washed out. They can also turn brown-green if they are cooked in slightly acidic water. This is because the remaining chlorophyll molecules lose their magnesium ions, which changes their colour. To stop this happening, some cooks add sodium hydrogencarbonate to the cooking water. It becomes slightly alkaline, allowing the magnesium ions to stay in the chlorophyll molecules. However, part of the chlorophyll molecule itself is lost this time, giving it an olive green colour. The cabbage looks more appetizing, but the alkali speeds up the **oxidation** of vitamin C in the food, which is not good for nutrition.

CHAPTER 6

Calcium

Calcium is a hard, silvery-white metal, but granules of it look dull grey because a thin layer of calcium oxide covers the surface. It reacts rapidly with cold water and acids, and it reacts violently with air when it is heated. Pure calcium has few industrial uses. However, **compounds** that contain calcium, particularly calcium carbonate and calcium oxide, are widely used in the manufacture of iron and steel, glass and cement. Our bones and teeth contain calcium, and calcium is an important **mineral** in our diet.

The discovery and isolation of calcium

Calcium is the fifth most abundant element in the Earth's crust and makes up about 3.6 per cent of it. Calcium compounds are found in many minerals, such as calcium carbonate in limestone, chalk and marble, calcium sulphate in gypsum, and calcium phosphate in phosphate rock. Calcium compounds have been in use for thousands of years. For instance, the Romans used calcium carbonate to make calcium oxide, which they used to mix concrete. However, calcium is not found naturally as a free metal. It was not isolated until 1808, when Sir Humphry Davy passed electricity through a mixture of molten calcium oxide and mercury oxide.

Extraction of calcium

The raw material for calcium production is calcium chloride, which is a by-product of the sodium carbonate industry. It can also be made by reacting hydrochloric acid with calcium carbonate from shells and rocks such as limestone. The calcium chloride is melted, and then electricity is passed through it. This causes calcium to form at the negative electrode, and chlorine gas to form at the positive electrode.

Pieces of calcium react rapidly with the air and rarely look shiny like this. ▶

Uses of calcium

Calcium is high up in the reactivity series (see page 17), so it can remove oxygen from the oxides of less reactive metals. For example, it is used to **extract** uranium from uranium oxide, and chromium from chromium oxides. In the same way, calcium is also used to remove oxygen and sulphur from metal **alloys**.

Calcium has proved a useful 'getter', which is a chemical that absorbs gases to maintain or improve the vacuum in a vacuum tube. Vacuum tubes are electronic components used in some specialist devices including radio and television transmitters. As much air as possible must be removed from them during manufacture so that they perform well.

Small amounts of calcium metal are mixed with other metals such as aluminium and magnesium to produce alloys with useful properties. For example, lead is a soft metal but it becomes much harder when even a very small amount of calcium is added to it. Lead-calcium alloys are used in bearings in machinery and to protect telephone cables from damage. Lead-calcium alloys containing about 0.1 per cent calcium are used in the lead plates found in car batteries. This is because they last longer and need less maintenance than plates made from other materials, such as lead-antimony alloy.

chalk

limestone

marble

▲ Limestone, chalk and marble are all forms of calcium carbonate.

Calcium carbonate

Calcium carbonate is a solid **compound** of calcium, carbon and oxygen. Living things in the oceans, such as snails and crabs, use carbon dioxide dissolved in the water to make calcium carbonate for their shells. Huge numbers of microscopic animals and plants called plankton also make their shells from calcium carbonate. When these living things die, they sink to the seabed and form layers of shells. The layers, called sediments, build up on top of each other. Their weight squeezes the water out from between the shells and they become stuck together by salt crystals. In this way, sedimentary rocks called limestone and chalk are formed over thousands of years. They can be nearly pure calcium carbonate.

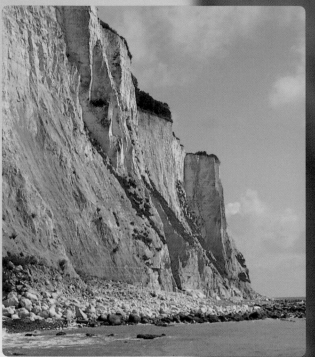

▲ *The white chalk cliffs in the south of England. The Latin word for chalk is 'creta', and the Cretaceous Period (66 to 144 million years ago) is named after the huge chalk deposits laid down during this time.*

Limestone

Limestone is a tough rock widely used for buildings, walls and paving stones. It contains crystals of calcium carbonate, varying in size from ones that are large enough to see, to microscopic crystals only a thousandth of a millimetre across. Limestone often also contains fossils of dead animals and plants that were trapped in the sediments as the rock formed. Crushed limestone is used in road building, and powdered limestone can be used to neutralize the acid in acidic lakes and rivers. Some limestones contain phosphates, so they are used to make **fertilizers**. One of the biggest uses of limestone is as a source of calcium oxide, which is used extensively in industry.

Chalk

Chalk is a white crumbly rock made almost entirely from microscopic shells, which makes it much softer than limestone. Builders use a piece of string rubbed in chalk to make straight lines on the ground and on building materials. Snooker players rub chalk on the end of their cues, and gymnasts and weight-lifters rub it into their hands to get a better grip. Chalk can be ground up to make a very fine powder called whiting. Putty is made from whiting mixed with a little linseed oil, and it is used to fill holes in woodwork and to seal glass into windows. Whiting is also used in crayons, rubber, paints and cosmetics. The chalk used by teachers to write on a chalkboard is not actually made from chalk, but from another calcium compound called calcium sulphate. Chalk is one of the raw materials used in the manufacture of cement and some fertilizers.

Marble

If limestone or chalk become buried deep underground by earth movements, they are put under pressure and heated without melting. Their crystal structure changes to form marble, which is a metamorphic rock. Marble is shiny, and harder than limestone or chalk. It can be polished to an attractive finish, so is used for statues, kitchen and bathroom surfaces and as a decorative cladding on buildings. Marble comes in different colours, but the most valuable form is white (statuary) marble, which is used by sculptors to create statues and sculptures.

This is the Taj Mahal in northern India. It is over 70 m high and was built from marble in the 17th century by more than 20,000 workers.

Limestone and limewater

When calcium oxide is added to water, it forms a solution of calcium hydroxide. This is often called limewater, and it is used to test for carbon dioxide gas. When calcium hydroxide and carbon dioxide react with each other, a cloudy white suspension of calcium carbonate forms in the limewater.

The word equation for the limewater test is:

calcium + carbon → calcium + water
hydroxide   dioxide   carbonate

This test is used to see if carbon dioxide is produced by a chemical **reaction**.

The limewater eventually becomes clear if more carbon dioxide is bubbled in. This is because a weak acid called carbonic acid forms and reacts with the calcium carbonate to make calcium hydrogencarbonate, which dissolves in water.

The word equation for the reaction between calcium carbonate and carbonic acid is:

calcium + carbonic →   calcium
carbonate   acid   hydrogencarbonate

This reaction causes huge caves to form, buildings to disintegrate and water to become hard.

Acid attack!

If you put a drop of hydrochloric acid on to a piece of limestone, chalk or marble, the rock fizzes and begins to disappear. This is because the calcium carbonate in the rock reacts with the acid. Rain is naturally acidic because carbon dioxide dissolves in it to make carbonic acid. Although it is a weak acid, rain and rivers that contain carbonic acid react with deposits of limestone and chalk. Over thousands of years, vast underground caves and channels can form in the rock.

◀ A limestone statue of a lion damaged by acid rain.

Fossil fuels such as coal and oil often contain sulphur. When these fuels are burnt, sulphur dioxide gas is produced, which dissolves in the clouds to form acid rain. In very badly polluted places the rain can be more acidic than lemon juice! If acid rain falls on buildings, statues and other stonework made from limestone, it attacks the stone and wears it away.

Stalactites and stalagmites

When water containing calcium hydrogencarbonate drips from the roof of caves, it evaporates to leave columns of solid calcium carbonate behind. These are called stalactites and stalagmites. Stalactites hang down from the ceiling, and stalagmites grow up from the floor. Sometimes they meet and form strange shapes, which some legends claim are the remains of witches!

The word equation for the production of a stalactite or stalagmite from a solution of calcium hydrogencarbonate is:

$$\text{calcium hydrogencarbonate} \rightarrow \text{calcium carbonate} + \text{water} + \text{carbon dioxide}$$

Solid calcium carbonate is left behind when the water evaporates and the carbon dioxide escapes into the atmosphere.

◀ Spectacular stalactites and stalagmites in Mitchell Caverns in California's Mojave National Scenic Area.

Calcium, hard water and health

It is usually easy to get soap to lather in soft water, but if you find it very difficult to get soap to lather, your water is hard. This does not mean that it is really tough, but that it contains dissolved magnesium and calcium **salts**. These get into the water if it flows over rocks such as limestone, chalk, gypsum or dolomite. The salts react with the fatty acids in soap to make a sticky grey-white scum, which makes it difficult to get you and your clothes clean. Even modern soapless detergents need higher temperatures and more detergent to get clothes clean than they do in soft water.

Hard water

Salts such as calcium sulphate cause permanent hardness. It is called permanent hardness because the water stays hard when it is boiled. Salts such as calcium hydrogencarbonate cause temporary hardness. It is called temporary hardness because the water becomes soft when it is boiled. This happens because the calcium hydrogencarbonate breaks down to form solid calcium carbonate. Unfortunately, the calcium carbonate builds up a spiky white 'scale' that damages kettles and irons. The scale that builds up inside boilers and hot water pipes can help to stop them corroding. However, if it gets too thick, the pipes can become so clogged up that they have to be replaced. Kettles and irons can be 'descaled' using acids to keep them working properly.

▼ *It is difficult to form a lather in hard water and a sticky scum forms. But soap easily forms a lather in soft water.*

Softening water

Sodium carbonate, also called washing soda, can soften water. It does this by reacting with the calcium salts to form solid calcium carbonate that does not interfere with soap. Washing powders often contain chemicals called phosphates. These stop the calcium salts in the water from reacting with soap, so improving the performance of the washing powder. Some homes in hard water areas may have **ion**-exchangers plumbed into their water supply. An ion-exchanger contains special beads that can swap sodium ions for calcium ions. As the water passes through, calcium ions from the dissolved calcium compounds stick on to the beads. Sodium ions come off them and dissolve in the water. Ion exchangers need to be recharged every so often by passing salty water through them.

Healthy hard water?

The dissolved salts in hard water give it a pleasant taste. Calcium is an important mineral in our diet, and hard water helps to supply it. Calcium is needed for our blood to clot properly, and to maintain healthy teeth and bones. It is needed for our muscles and nerves to work properly, and there is some evidence that people living in hard water areas suffer fewer heart attacks than those living in areas with soft water.

Water is an important part of our diet and we should drink at least 2 litres a day. Hard water also contains calcium salts that help to keep our teeth and bones healthy.

Bones

Without a skeleton, we would be floppy and would look very different. The skeleton does many important jobs, including supporting the body, giving it a shape and allowing the muscles to move it. It also protects vital organs inside it, such as the lungs and brain. Our skeleton is called an endoskeleton because it is inside our body, and it is made from bone. There is about 1 kg of calcium in a typical 70 kg person, and about 99 per cent of this is stored in the bones.

Strong but flexible

Bones need to be strong enough to carry the weight of a body without being squashed or bent. Cells called osteoblasts inside the bone produce crystals of a hard **mineral** called hydroxylapatite. This is a type of calcium phosphate, and makes up over half the weight of the bone. Bones must also be flexible to prevent them from snapping easily when bent or pulled. Bones get their flexibility from a tough elastic protein inside them called collagen. Bones are made from a 'composite material' – they contain two different types of material and get the best out of both. Hydroxylapatite is strong when squashed but easily snapped, whereas collagen is strong when stretched or bent, but easily squashed.

▼ *The top chicken bone was heated in an oven for half an hour leaving the minerals behind, and the one below was soaked in vinegar overnight to dissolve out the minerals. The bone from the oven snaps easily, but the one soaked in vinegar is soft and floppy.*

Astronauts and old age

Calcium is constantly moving in and out of our bones, depending on our diet and on how we use our bodies. Osteoblasts produce hydroxylapatite but other cells called osteoclasts remove it. Bone builds up where more hydroxylapatite is produced than is removed. This usually happens in bone put under pressure from exercise. Bone becomes weaker where more hydroxylapatite is removed than is produced. This usually happens in bone that is not put under pressure, for example through lack of exercise. It is natural for bone to change like this throughout our life.

Astronauts in space are weightless, so their bones are not under pressure. Their bones quickly lose hydroxylapatite, which limits how long astronauts can spend in space. As we get older, hydroxylapatite is eventually lost from our bones faster than it is replaced. This is part of the natural ageing process, but some old people lose so much hydroxylapatite that they get osteoporosis. Their bones become weak and easily broken, and they become shorter and bent over.

Eat well and exercise

Calcium is an important mineral in our diet. It is found in foods such as milk, cheese and tofu. If we do not get enough calcium in our diet, we run the risk of getting weak bones and teeth (which also contain calcium). Vitamin D is important for controlling the levels of calcium and phosphorus in our bodies. Children who do not get enough vitamin D can develop rickets, which causes their legs to become curved. Eggs, butter and margarine are good sources of vitamin D, and our bodies can also make it when we play outside in the sunshine.

◀ *This X-ray shows the bowed legs of a child suffering from rickets.*

Calcium oxide

If calcium carbonate is heated strongly, it decomposes or breaks down to form calcium oxide and carbon dioxide. Calcium oxide is also called lime or quicklime. It is a base, meaning it can react with acids and neutralize them. Farmers spread calcium oxide on their fields to neutralize excess acid in the soil, but it has many industrial uses.

*The word equation for the **decomposition** of calcium carbonate is:*

$$\text{calcium carbonate} \xrightarrow{\text{heat}} \text{calcium oxide} + \text{carbon dioxide}$$

Iron and blast furnace

Iron is **extracted** from iron **ore** in a huge steel column called a blast furnace, which is lined with heat-resistant bricks to stop it melting in the heat. The raw materials needed are iron ore, coke and limestone. Hot air is blasted into the bottom of the furnace to burn the coke, eventually producing carbon monoxide. This reacts with the iron ore to make molten iron. However, the molten iron contains sandy impurities from the original iron ore. These must be removed from the iron, a process in which limestone is used.

Calcium oxide gives off very bright 'limelight' when it is heated by the flame from a mixture of oxygen and hydrogen.

In the heat of the blast furnace, the limestone decomposes to form calcium oxide and carbon dioxide. The calcium oxide reacts with the sandy impurities to make a molten slag. This floats on the surface of the iron, and is easily removed to leave purified iron behind.

The word equation for the production of slag in the blast furnace is:

calcium oxide + silicon dioxide ⟶ calcium silicate

Sand is mostly silica, or silicon dioxide. This reacts with the calcium oxide from the limestone to produce a calcium silicate slag.

Cooled and solidified slag can be used in road building. Glassy granules are made if the slag is cooled very quickly with jets of water. These granules are ground to a fine powder, which is used in the manufacture of strong, fire-resistant concrete.

Cement and concrete
When heated, the calcium carbonate in chalk breaks down to produce calcium oxide and carbon dioxide. Cement is made by strongly heating a mixture of chalk and clay. If cement, sand, aggregate (small stones) and water are mixed together, concrete is made. Enough concrete is used around the world to provide everyone on the planet with a tonne each year! Mortar (used by builders to join bricks together to make walls) is made by mixing calcium oxide with sand and water.

Glass making
Glass can be made by melting sand, then cooling it very quickly. Sand melts at 1700 °C, a heat that requires a lot of energy. To reduce the energy needed, glass manufacturers add sodium carbonate. This breaks down in the heat to form sodium oxide, which reduces the melting temperature to 800 °C. Unfortunately, it makes glass that dissolves in water! To prevent this, calcium carbonate is also added, which forms calcium oxide in the glass. About 90 per cent of glass is this soda-lime glass or bottle glass.

More calcium compounds

Coal-fired power stations, and some industries, produce sulphur dioxide gas as a by-product. This will cause acid rain if it is allowed to escape into the atmosphere. One of the methods to stop it escaping uses powdered calcium oxide. This reacts with the sulphur dioxide to produce a useful **compound** called calcium sulphate, which is used in toothpaste, lipstick and blackboard chalk.

The word equation for using calcium oxide to remove sulphur dioxide is:

calcium oxide + sulphur dioxide + oxygen → calcium sulphate

Gypsum and plaster of Paris

Gypsum is a sedimentary rock that contains calcium sulphate, $CaSO_4$. Powdered gypsum is used widely for plaster and plasterboard to line walls and ceilings in buildings. The crystals of calcium sulphate in gypsum contain a small amount of water. Plaster of Paris is made by heating gypsum to 100 °C to remove the water from it. When water is added back to plaster of Paris, it warms slightly, expands and then sets hard. Dentists use it to make casts of teeth, and artists use it to make moulds for their works of art. Forensic scientists use plaster of Paris to make a permanent record of shoe or tyre prints left behind at the scene of a crime. Plaster of Paris casts are used to hold broken bones still while they mend.

▲ *Dentists use plaster of Paris when making moulds of their patients' teeth.*

Fertilizers and flames

Plants need **minerals** to grow properly, especially nitrogen, phosphorus and potassium. Artificial **fertilizers** are often added to the soil to provide these minerals. Phosphate rock contains calcium phosphate. This would make a good source of phosphorus for plants, but unfortunately it does not dissolve in water. As a result, plants cannot absorb it through their roots, so fertilizer manufacturers convert it to ammonium phosphate, which does dissolve in water.

Calcium carbide, CaC_2, is a manufactured grey solid that reacts vigorously with water. The **reaction** produces calcium hydroxide, $Ca(OH)_2$, and ethyne, C_2H_2. This is a very flammable gas that is also called acetylene. It is used as the fuel in oxy-acetylene **welding** and cutting torches to produce a very hot flame.

Calcium chloride

Calcium chloride, $CaCl_2$, is a useful waste **product** from the sodium carbonate industry. It absorbs moisture, so the oil industry uses calcium chloride to dry oil fractions, and chemists use it in their experiments if they want to remove moisture from the air. It is also used as a food additive – it absorbs water and keeps the food firm.

Calcium chloride is used to remove snow and ice from roads in the winter. When **salts** such as calcium chloride are mixed with ice, they lower the melting point of the ice, causing it to melt. Calcium chloride works particularly well, right down to −31 °C, because heat is released when it dissolves in water.

◀ *Grit and calcium chloride are spread on roads to prevent ice and snow building up in winter.*

CHAPTER 7

Strontium

Strontium is a soft, silvery-white metal. When exposed to the air it quickly reacts with oxygen to form a layer of strontium oxide, SrO, which has a yellowish colour. To prevent it doing this, strontium is usually stored under oil, just like the **group** 1 metals. Strontium carbonate is used widely in the manufacture of glass for television tubes but, in general, strontium **compounds** have few industrial uses. This is because they have very similar properties to compounds containing calcium or barium, but are more expensive.

The discovery and isolation of strontium

Adair Crawford and William Cruickshank discovered strontium in 1790 when they studied a **mineral** from a lead mine near Strontian in Scotland. At first they thought that the mineral was witherite, which contains barium carbonate, but they were able to show that it was quite different. They called the new mineral strontianite, which we now know contains strontium carbonate. Crawford and Cruickshank knew that strontianite contained a new metal, but they could not isolate it. Sir Humphry Davy managed to isolate strontium eighteen years later by passing electricity through a mixture of molten strontium chloride and mercury oxide.

▲ *Crystals of celestite, strontium sulphate. Celestite is used to make strontium nitrate, which gives the red colour in fireworks and tracer bullets.*

Extraction of strontium

Strontium is quite rare in the Earth's crust and makes up about 0.045 per cent of it. Minerals such as strontianite and celestite (strontium sulphate) contain strontium, but it is never found naturally as a free metal. About half a million tonnes of strontium minerals are mined in the world each year, mostly in China, Mexico and Spain. Very little strontium metal is made commercially because it is very similar to calcium and barium, which are more widely available. Strontium is **extracted** by the **electrolysis** of a mixture of molten strontium chloride and potassium chloride. When electricity is passed through the mixture, strontium metal forms at the negative electrode and chlorine gas forms at the positive electrode.

Uses of strontium

More than three-quarters of the strontium produced is used to make glass for cathode ray tubes. These are used in televisions and computer monitors, and they produce small amounts of X-rays as part of their normal operation. Strontium carbonate, $SrCO_3$ is added to the molten glass while it is being made. It breaks down in the heat to produce carbon dioxide and strontium oxide, SrO, which absorbs X-rays when the cathode ray tube is used. Flat panel displays work differently to cathode ray tubes, so the demand for strontium is likely to go down as they become more popular.

Strontium hydroxide, $Sr(OH)_2$, reacts with fatty acids from oils to make substances called metallic soaps. These do not dissolve easily in water, and are used in the manufacture of thick, waterproof greases. Strontium chloride, $SrCl_2$, or strontium ethanoate, $(CH_3COO)_2Sr$, are the active ingredients in toothpastes for sensitive teeth. Tiny liquid-filled holes in the teeth, called tubules, can connect to nerves. This can make teeth sensitive to hot drinks and cold foods. The strontium **compounds** block these tubules, reducing the sensitivity of the teeth.

Strontium carbonate is used in the manufacture of glass for television sets and computer monitors. As widescreen televisions become more popular, the demand for strontium is likely to go up.

Radioactive strontium

In the middle of the last century, nuclear weapons were tested above ground. These 'atmospheric tests' produced a lot of **radioactive** fallout, which contained dangerous radioactive **isotopes**. These were carried around the world by the wind and found their way into the water and soil. One of the more dangerous radioactive isotopes was strontium-90.

Isotopes

Isotopes are **atoms** of an **element** that have the same number of **protons** and **electrons**, but different numbers of **neutrons**. There are four natural isotopes of strontium, but strontium-88 is the most abundant or common. It makes up 82.6 per cent of natural strontium. It has 38 protons and 50 neutrons in its **nucleus**, and it is given the chemical symbol ^{88}Sr.

Radiation

The atoms of the four natural strontium isotopes are stable, which means that they do not break up into smaller pieces. However, the atoms of some isotopes are unstable, which means that they can break up or **decay** into smaller pieces. When they do so, they become another isotope of the same element, or an isotope of another element. They also give out **radiation**.

There are different types of radiation. Depending on the type of radiation produced, it can pass through the air, plastic and metal, and into our bodies. If radiation damages the DNA in our cells, it can lead to cancer. To prevent this, there are strict laws to protect us from over-exposure to radioactive chemicals. Strontium-90 (^{90}Sr) emits powerful **beta radiation**, which consists of fast-moving electrons fired out of the nucleus as it decays.

Half-life

Nobody can predict when an individual atom will decay. However, if scientists study huge numbers of atoms, they can say how long it would take for half of them to decay. The time it takes for half of the atoms to decay is called the

half-life of the isotope. Some stable isotopes have half-lives of thousands or millions of years, but some unstable isotopes can have half-lives of only a fraction of a second. Strontium-90 is the most stable artificial isotope of strontium, with a half-life of 28.1 years. It is an artificial isotope because it is made in nuclear **reactions** and does not occur naturally.

▼ *Different types of radiation can go through different types of materials. **Alpha radiation** is stopped by paper; beta radiation is stopped by sheets of aluminium; and **gamma radiation** is stopped by very thick sheets of lead.*

Strontium-90

Strontium and calcium are chemically very similar, and the cells of plants and animals cannot easily tell them apart. This means that plants and animals absorb strontium, which can be dangerous if some of it is strontium-90 from nuclear fallout. If strontium-90 contaminates food, such as milk, it can become concentrated in bones and teeth, where its radiation may cause leukaemia and bone cancer.

It is not all bad news for strontium-90, as it is used in some luminous signs. Heat is produced as it decays, and this can be converted into electricity in a nuclear battery. These batteries are used to supply electricity over a long period of time in difficult places such as weather stations in remote areas, navigation buoys at sea and space probes.

CHAPTER 8

Barium

Barium is a soft, silvery-white metal that is slightly harder than lead. When barium is exposed to the air it quickly reacts with oxygen to form a layer of barium oxide. To stop it doing this, it is usually stored under oil or in an unreactive atmosphere such as argon gas. Barium metal has very few uses, and many barium **compounds** are poisonous – barium carbonate is used as rat poison. Chemists use barium chloride to detect sulphates in chemicals, and barium nitrate is used to produce an apple green flame for fireworks and signal flares.

The discovery and isolation of barium

In 1774, a Swedish chemist, Carl Scheele, discovered barium when he studied a **mineral** called pyrolusite. Scheele was able to show that it contained a new compound, which we now know is barium oxide. He was unable to isolate the metal, but he managed to make barium sulphate crystals by reacting the barium oxide with sulphuric acid. He sent some of the crystals to his friend Johan Gahn, a fellow Swede. In 1775, Gahn showed that a mineral called barite contained barium sulphate, but he could not isolate barium either.

Sir Humphry Davy managed to isolate barium in 1808 when he passed electricity through a mixture of molten barium oxide and mercury oxide. He named the metal barium, from the Greek word for 'heavy'. This was because minerals containing barium, such as barite, have a high **density** compared to many other minerals. However, barium itself has quite a low density, just a third more than aluminium. This meant that some chemists complained about the name, but it became too late to change it.

*Crystals of white barite, barium sulphate. ▶
Barite is the main **ore** of barium. It is
used in special X-rays as barium meals
and enemas. It is also used in oil, paper
and rubber industries.*

English chemist, Sir Humphry Davy, discovered sodium and potassium in 1807, and a year later he became the first person to isolate barium, magnesium, calcium and strontium

Extraction of barium

Barium is quite rare in the Earth's crust and makes up about 0.04 per cent of it. Barium is never found naturally as a free metal, but it is contained in minerals like witherite (barium carbonate) and barite. Over two million tonnes of these minerals are mined in the world each year, mostly in the USA, Denmark and France. Like the other **alkaline** earth metals, barium is **extracted** by **electrolysis**. When electricity is passed through molten barium chloride, barium metal forms at the negative electrode and chlorine gas forms at the positive electrode.

Uses of barium

Barium is a very reactive metal, so barium and barium-aluminium alloys are used as 'getters' to remove traces of gases such as oxygen from vacuum tubes. These are electronic components used in some specialist devices, and they will not work if they contain even small amounts of gas.

The word equation for barium removing oxygen from a vacuum tube is:

$$barium + oxygen \rightarrow barium\ oxide$$

A tiny amount of solid barium oxide is formed.

Barium-nickel alloys give off **electrons** easily when they are heated. They are used in spark plugs to ignite the fuel in car engines, and in the cathode ray tubes used for television sets and computer monitors.

Barium compounds

Chemists sometimes need to find out if a liquid contains dissolved sulphates. To do this, they add a few drops of barium chloride, $BaCl_2$, solution to the liquid. If there are any sulphates in the liquid, they form barium sulphate, $BaSO_4$. This is a white solid that does not dissolve in water, so the mixture turns cloudy white. Barium sulphate and other barium **compounds** are useful in industry, too.

The word equation for the test for a sulphate is:

$$\text{sodium} + \text{barium} \longrightarrow \text{sodium} + \text{barium}$$
$$\text{sulphate} \quad \text{chloride} \qquad \text{chloride} \quad \text{sulphate}$$

*In this example, sodium sulphate is detected. Barium sulphate does not dissolve in water and forms a white **precipitate**. A few drops of hydrochloric acid are usually added as well to stop other barium compounds forming, which would spoil the result.*

Paint and barium meals

Barite is a **mineral** that contains barium sulphate. Powdered barite is often used as a **filler** in the manufacture of rubber, plastics and paper. Fillers are substances added to materials to make them cheaper or stiffer. It can also be mixed with mud to make a dense liquid called slurry. This is used to lubricate the cutting bits used to drill oil wells.

White paint used to contain lead carbonate, which is poisonous. An alternative called lithopone was developed near the end of the 19th century. To make it, barium sulphate and zinc sulphide are mixed together and heated strongly for a long time. Lithopone was widely used as the white pigment in paints and face powder. However, it has largely been replaced by titanium dioxide, which is cheaper.

X-rays do not easily pass though barium, so barium sulphate mixed with water is used in X-ray examinations of the

This barium X-ray shows a healthy small intestine. In the past, surgeons would have had to operate in order to see what was happening in the body. Today X-rays like this help them to diagnose first.

stomach and intestines. If the patient swallows the mixture it is called a 'barium meal', and if it is passed into their rectum through a tube it is called a 'barium enema'. When the radiologist takes an X-ray photograph of the patient, their stomach or intestines show up white wherever the barium sulphate has gone. Barium sulphate is not absorbed through the intestines, and it leaves the body when the patient goes to the toilet.

Glass and rat poison

The cathode ray tubes used in television sets produce small amounts of X-rays as part of their normal operation. Barium oxide, BaO, can be added to the glass to absorb the X-rays. When the glass is being made, it is mixed with barium carbonate, $BaCO_3$. This breaks down in the heat to produce carbon dioxide and the required barium oxide.

Barium carbonate is used in rat poison! It is not poisonous immediately because, like barium sulphate, it does not dissolve in water. However, once it is in the rat's stomach, the barium carbonate reacts with the hydrochloric acid there to form barium chloride. This does dissolve in water and passes through the rat's intestines to poison it. The same would happen to a human, so it is best avoided.

Radium

Radium is a rare, silvery-white metal. It is the most reactive alkaline earth metal. Not only does it react with oxygen in the air to form radium oxide, RaO, it reacts rapidly with nitrogen to form a black coating of radium nitride, Ra_3N_2. Radium is intensely **radioactive** and glows in the dark, but it has no practical applications in our everyday lives. In the last century, however, radium had many uses. It was used to make luminous paints for watch dials, and in cancer treatments. It was even used in some very strange potions sold by bogus doctors until the dangers of **radiation** were fully understood.

The discovery and isolation of radium

Marie Curie was a Polish-French scientist who was born in 1867. While studying uranium and its **ore**, pitchblende, she discovered that the pitchblende was more radioactive than the uranium itself. She realized that there had to be other **elements** in the pitchblende that were more radioactive than uranium. Marie set out to isolate these elements from pitchblende with help from her husband, Pierre. In 1898, they managed to produce two tiny fractions of intensely radioactive material. One fraction contained an element that they called polonium, after Poland where Marie was born. The other fraction contained another element that was even more radioactive than polonium. They called it radium, after the Latin word for ray.

Marie Curie and André Debierne set out to isolate some radium from a tonne of pitchblende. By 1910, they had managed to **extract** about a tenth of a gram of radium. They used **electrolysis** to do this, just as Humphry Davy had done with the other **alkaline** earth metals over a hundred years earlier.

A photograph of Marie and Pierre Curie ▶
taken in their laboratory in 1903.

▲ This is a sample of uranium ore called pitchblende. The yellow-orange areas are uranium hydroxide (gummite) and the darker areas are uranium oxide (uraninite). Pitchblende contains tiny amounts of uranium.

Extraction of radium

Radium is only formed by the radioactive **decay** of other elements, such as uranium. Consequently, it is rarely found in the Earth's crust. However, it is concentrated in uranium ores, such as pitchblende and carnotite from the USA, Canada, Australia and the Democratic Republic of the Congo. Even so, one tonne of ore can produce as little as 0.15 g of radium, and only about 100 g of radium is produced in the world each year. As radium is very reactive chemically, it is usually supplied as radium chloride, $RaCl_2$, or radium bromide, $RaBr_2$. These **compounds** are more stable chemically than the metal itself, which is extracted from radium chloride by electrolysis if it is needed.

Radium and radioactivity

Radium is about two million times more radioactive than uranium, and its uses rely on its intense radioactivity. There are over 30 radium **isotopes**, with **half-life** ranges from 1600 years for radium-226 to less than two millionths of a second for radium-217. The modern unit of radioactivity is the becquerel (Bq), one radioactive decay per second. The old unit of radioactivity was the Curie, the same amount of radioactivity as 1 g of radium-226 (37 billion Bq).

Uses of radium

Radium gives off powerful **radiation** as it **decays**. The dangers of this were not known when radium was discovered. Marie Curie was fascinated by the way her laboratory glassware glowed in the dark at night because of the traces of radium on it, and Pierre Curie used to carry radium around in his waistcoat pocket. The radiation caused a large sore patch on his chest, but it did not kill him – a heavy horse-drawn cart did that in 1906. Marie Curie died of leukaemia in 1934, most probably caused by exposure to radiation.

Radiation and cancer treatment

Although exposure to radium may cause cancer, the radiation can be used to kill cancer cells if it is carefully controlled. Radium was widely used in the last century for radiotherapy, which is the treatment of cancer using radiation. Marie Curie herself worked very hard to research radium and to promote its use in radiotherapy. In 1920 she started the Curie Foundation to raise money for the Radium Institute in Paris. During a tour of the USA a year later, the President presented her with a gram of radium. To pay for it, the American Association of University Women had raised $156,413 – which was then an enormous amount of money. The gift doubled the amount of radium the Institute had for its scientific and medical research! However, modern radiotherapy uses cheaper and safer sources, such as cobalt-60.

Luminous dials

Zinc sulphide glows in the dark, but a mixture of zinc sulphide and radium glows even more brightly. It was this mixture that was first used in luminous paints. Although radium was very expensive, very little was needed because it is so very radioactive. As a result, in the early part of the last century all sorts of objects were painted with radium paints, including the hands of watches, instrument dials and even buttons. Unfortunately, the women who applied the paint in factories suffered from the effects of radiation, and many of them became ill with cancer. As a result, radium is no longer used for luminous paints.

Amazing but true!

Despite the growing understanding at the start of the last century about the dangers of radiation, all sorts of strange products containing radium were sold to an eager and unsuspecting public during the 1920s and 1930s. As it decays, radium produces radon gas. Among other claims, radon was believed to improve health and kill germs, and people thought that radium would be even more effective. Radioactive water containing radium was very fashionable as a tonic. People even made their own radioactive water using containers lined with radioactive **minerals**. Bandages and pads containing radium were popular 'treatments' to ease the joint pain of rheumatism and arthritis, and other products containing radium included soap, toothpaste and skin creams! Inevitably, many people fell seriously ill and the craze for radium ended. Modern products like these do not contain radium, and will have been tested rigorously to avoid any risks to health.

CRÈME SCIENTIFIQUE

CURATIVE EMBELLISSANTE

THO-RADIA
à base de thorium et de radium selon la formule du
DOCTEUR ALFRED CURIE
EN VENTE EXCLUSIVEMENT CHEZ LES PHARMACIENS

◀ This 1933 advertisement is for a facial cream containing radium and thorium. Even scientists were unaware of how dangerous these substances were. One year later, Marie Curie died from leukaemia from her work with radioactive elements.

Find out more about the alkaline earth metals

Elements

The table below contains some information about the properties of the **alkaline** earth metals.

Element	Symbol	Atomic number	Melting point (°C)	Boiling point (°C)	Density (g/cm3)
beryllium	Be	4	1287	2469	1.85
magnesium	Mg	12	650	1090	1.74
calcium	Ca	20	842	1484	1.55
strontium	Sr	38	777	1382	2.63
barium	Ba	56	727	1870	3.51
radium	Ra	88	700	1737	5.00

Compounds

These tables show you the chemical formulas of most of the **compounds** mentioned in the book. For example, calcium carbonate has the formula $CaCO_3$. This means it is made from one calcium **atom**, one carbon atom and three oxygen atoms, joined together by chemical **bonds**. Nearly all these compounds are solid at room temperature.

Barium compounds

Barium compounds	formula
barium carbonate	$BaCO_3$
barium chlorate	$Ba(ClO)_2$
barium chloride	$BaCl_2$
barium nitrate	$Ba(NO_3)_2$
barium oxide	BaO
barium sulphate	$BaSO_4$

Beryllium compounds

Beryllium compounds	formula
beryllium aluminium silicate	$Be_3Al_2(SiO_3)_6$
beryllium chloride	$BeCl_2$
beryllium fluoride	BeF_2
beryllium oxide	BeO

Calcium compounds	formula
calcium carbide	CaC_2
calcium carbonate	$CaCO_3$
calcium chloride	$CaCl_2$
calcium hydrogencarbonate	$CaHCO_3$
calcium hydroxide	$Ca(OH)_2$
calcium hydroxyphosphate	$Ca_{10}(PO_4)_6(OH)_2$
calcium hypochlorite	$Ca(ClO)_2$
calcium nitride	Ca_3N_2
calcium oxide	CaO
calcium phosphate	$Ca_3(PO_4)_2$
calcium silicate	$CaSiO_3$
calcium sulphate	$CaSO_4$
hydroxylapatite	$Ca_{10}(PO_4)_6(OH)_2$

Magnesium compounds	formula
magnesium carbonate	$MgCO_3$
magnesium chloride	$MgCl_2$
magnesium fluoride	MgF_2
magnesium hydroxide	$Mg(OH)_2$
magnesium nitrate	$Mg(NO_3)_2$
magnesium oxide	MgO
magnesium sulphate	$MgSO_4$
magnesium sulphide	MgS

Radium of compounds	formula
radium bromide	$RaBr_2$
radium chloride	$RaCl_2$
carnotite	$K_2(UO_2)_2V_2O_8$
pitchblende	UO_2 and UO_3

Find out more continued

Acids

Acids	formula
phosphoric acid	H_3PO_4
sulphuric acid	H_2SO_4
vitamin C (ascorbic acid)	$C_6H_8O_6$

Strontium compounds

Strontium compounds	formula
strontium carbonate	$SrCO_3$
strontium chloride	$SrCl_2$
strontium ethanoate	$(CH_3COO)_2Sr$
strontium hydroxide	$Sr(OH)_2$
strontium nitrate	$Sr(NO_3)_2$
strontium oxide	SrO
strontium sulphate	$SrSO_4$

Other compounds

Other compounds	formula
carbon dioxide (gas)	CO_2
copper nitrate	$Cu(NO_3)_2$
ethyne (gas)	C_2H_2
mercury oxide	HgO
potassium chloride	KCl
potassium hydroxide	KOH
silicon dioxide	SiO_2
sodium carbonate	Na_2CO_3
sodium chloride	$NaCl$
sodium hexafluorosilicate	Na_2SiF_6
sodium hydrogencarbonate	$NaHCO_3$
uranium tetrafluoride	UF_4
water (liquid)	H_2O

Glossary

alkaline liquid with a pH above 7. When a base such as calcium hydroxide dissolves in water, it makes an alkaline solution.

alpha radiation (α radiation) radiation caused by quickly moving helium nuclei that have broken away from an unstable nucleus

alloy mixture of two or more metals, or mixture of a metal and a non-metal. Alloys are often more useful than the pure metal on its own.

atom smallest particle of an element that has the property of that element. Atoms contain smaller particles called sub-atomic particles.

atomic number number of protons in the nucleus of an atom. It is also called the proton number. No two elements have the same atomic number.

beta radiation (β radiation) radiation consisting of fast-moving electrons produced by an unstable nucleus when it breaks up

bond the force that joins atoms together

brittle the word that describes a solid that breaks into small pieces when hit. Glass is a brittle solid.

catalyst substance that speeds up reactions without getting used up

compound substance made from the atoms of two or more elements, joined together by chemical bonds. Compounds can be broken down into simpler substances, and they have different properties from the elements in them. For example, water is a liquid at room temperature, but it is made from two gases, hydrogen and oxygen.

decay when the nucleus of a radioactive substance breaks up, giving off radiation and becoming the nucleus of another element, it decays

decomposition type of chemical reaction where a compound breaks down into simpler substances, such as the elements in them. For example, water can decompose to make hydrogen and oxygen.

density mass of a substance compared to its volume. To work out the density of a substance, you divide its mass by its volume. Substances with a high density feel very heavy for their size.

displace when one element takes the place of another element in a compound

electrolysis breaking down or decomposing a compound by passing electricity through it. The compound must be molten or dissolved in a liquid for electrolysis to work.

electron sub-atomic particle with a negative electric charge. Electrons are found around the nucleus of an atom.

element substance made from one type of atom. Elements cannot be broken down into simpler substances. All substances are made from one or more elements.

enzyme catalyst made by living things. Enzymes are made from proteins, and control the chemical reactions that happen in living things.

extract to remove a chemical from a mixture of chemicals

fertilizer chemicals that give plants the elements they need for healthy growth

filler substance added to a product to make it cheaper or to improve its properties

gamma radiation (γ radiation) powerful radiation caused by very high frequency light waves. Gamma radiation cannot be seen and it can pass through metal.

groups vertical columns of elements in the periodic table. Elements in a group have similar properties.

half-life the time taken for half the atoms of a radioactive substance to decay

ion a charged particle made when atoms lose or gain electrons. If a metal atom loses electrons it becomes a positive ion. If a non-metal atom gains electrons it becomes a negative ion.

isotope atoms of an element with the same number of protons and electrons, but different numbers of neutrons. Isotopes share the same atomic number but they have a different mass number.

mass number in the nucleus of an atom, the number of protons added to the number of neutrons

metal hydroxide compounds containing metal ions and hydroxide ions (OH^-)

mineral substance that is found naturally but does not come from animals or plants. Metal ores and limestone are examples of minerals.

molecule smallest particle of an element or compound that exists by itself. A molecule is usually made from two or more atoms joined together.

neutralization reaction between an acid and an alkali or a base. The solution made is neutral, which means it is not acidic or alkaline.

neutron sub-atomic particle with no electric charge. Neutrons are found in the nucleus of an atom.

nucleus part of an atom made from protons and neutrons. It has a positive electric charge and is found at the centre of the atom.

ore mineral from which metal can be taken out and purified

oxidation adding of oxygen to an element or compound in a chemical reaction. For example, carbon is oxidized when it reacts with oxygen to make carbon dioxide.

period horizontal row of elements in the periodic table

periodic table table in which all the known elements are arranged into groups and period

photosynthesis chemical reaction that green plants use to make sugars from carbon dioxide and water using the energy from light. Oxygen is also made.

precipitate solid that appears when two solutions are mixed

product substance made in a chemical reaction

proton sub-atomic particle with a positive electric charge. Protons are found in the nucleus of an atom

proton number the number of protons in the nucleus of an atom. It is also called the atomic number. No two elements have the same proton number.

radioactive substance that can produce radiation

radiation energy or particles given off when an atom decays

reaction chemical change that produces new substances

salt compound formed when an acid is neutralized by a base

sub-atomic particle particle smaller than an atom, such as proton, neutron and electron

welding joining two or more metals together, usually by heating them

Timeline

calcium and magnesium discovered	1755	Joseph Black
barium discovered	1774	Carl Scheele
strontium discovered	1790	Adair Crawford and William Cruickshank
calcium isolated	1808	Sir Humphry Davy
barium isolated	1808	Sir Humphry Davy
strontium isolated	1808	Sir Humphry Davy
magnesium isolated	1808	Sir Humphry Davy
beryllium isolated	1828	Antione-Alexandre-Brutus Bussy and Friedrich Wöhler
radium discovered	1898	Marie Curie and Pierre Curie
radium isolated	1910	Marie Curie and André Debierne

Further reading and useful websites

Books

Fullick, Ann, *Science Topics: Chemicals in Action* (Heinemann Library, 1999)

Knapp, Brian, *The Elements* series, particularly, *Calcium and Magnesium* (Atlantic Europe Publishing Co., 1996)

Oxlade, Chris, *Chemicals in Action* series, particularly *Atoms; Elements and Compounds* (Heinemann Library, 2002)

Websites

WebElements™
http://www.webelements.com
An interactive periodic table crammed with information and photographs.

DiscoverySchool
http://school.discovery.com/students
Help for science projects and homework, and free science clip art.

Proton Don
http://www.funbrain.com/periodic
The fun periodic table quiz!

BBC Science
http://www.bbc.co.uk/science
Quizzes, news, information and games about all areas of science.

Creative Chemistry
http://www.creative-chemistry.org.uk
An interactive chemistry site with fun practical activities, quizzes, puzzles, etc.

Mineralogy Database
http://www.webmineral.com
Lots of useful information about minerals, including colour photographs and information about their chemistry.

Index

acid rain 36, 37, 44
acids 12-13, 24, 28, 34, 36, 60
aircraft and spacecraft parts 8, 22, 23
alkaline earth metals 7, 8, 12, 18
alloys 8, 9, 22, 23, 24, 26, 27, 33, 51
aluminium 17, 23, 27, 33
atomic numbers 6, 7, 58
atoms 4-5, 10, 16, 17, 22, 48

barium 7, 8, 11, 15, 19, 50-3, 58
barium sulphate 11, 52-3, 58
batteries 18, 19, 24, 33, 49
beryllium 5, 7, 8, 12, 14, 17, 19, 20-3, 58
blast furnaces 28, 42, 43
bones and teeth 9, 32, 39, 40-1, 49

calcium 4, 7, 8, 9, 12, 14, 15, 17, 19, 32-45, 49, 58, 59
calcium carbonate 9, 32, 34-7, 42, 43, 59
calcium chloride 32, 45, 59
calcium oxide 12, 25, 32, 34, 36, 42-3, 44, 59
calcium sulphate 35, 44, 59
cancer treatment 56
catalysts 23, 30
cathode ray tubes 47, 51, 53
cement 9, 29, 43
chalk 9, 32, 34, 35, 36, 38, 43
chlorophyll 31
compounds 4, 8, 9, 10, 20, 23, 28-9, 32, 34-8, 42-5, 46, 50, 52-3, 55, 58-60
concrete 9, 43

densities 24, 27, 50, 58
diet 9, 30, 32, 39, 41

drying agents 29, 45
duralumin 27

electricity 18, 24, 49
electrolysis 18-19, 24, 25, 47, 51, 54
electrons 5, 6, 16, 17, 30, 48, 51
elements 4, 6-7, 18, 58
emeralds 8, 20, 21, 23
enzymes 30
Epsom Salt 29

fertilizers 29, 34, 35, 45
flame retardants 29
flares and fireworks 9, 10, 11, 28

glass 10, 43, 46, 47, 53
gypsum 32, 38, 44

hard water 38-9
hydrogen 12, 13, 14, 15, 18
hydroxylapatite 40, 41

ion exchanger 39
ions 25, 30, 31, 39
iron and steel 9, 26, 27, 42, 43
irritants 9, 15
isolation of the elements 18-19, 20, 24, 46, 50, 54
isotopes 10, 48, 49, 55

limestone 9, 32, 34, 36, 37, 38

magnesium 4, 7, 8, 9, 12, 13, 14, 15, 16, 17, 19, 24-31, 58, 59
magnesium chloride 13, 25, 29, 59
magnesium hydroxide 9, 14, 25, 28-9, 59
magnesium oxide 4, 9, 12, 15, 24, 28, 59
magnesium sulphate 13, 29, 59

marble 9, 32, 35, 36
melting and boiling points 9, 22, 58
metal hydroxides 14
metal oxides 12, 33
metallic soaps 47
Milk of Magnesia 9, 28

noble gases 16
nuclear reactors 22

oxy-acetylene welding 45
oxygen 4, 12, 18, 20, 24, 28, 31, 33, 54

periodic table 5, 6-7
photosynthesis 31
pitchblende 54, 55, 59
plaster of Paris 9, 44
poisonous metals and compounds 8, 11, 20, 50
potassium 19, 20, 21, 45

radiation 10, 11, 12, 22, 48, 49, 54, 55, 56, 57
radiotherapy 56
radium 4, 7, 8, 11, 12, 17, 19, 54-7, 58, 59
reactivity series 17, 33
refractory bricks 28
rust 26-7

sacrificial protection 27
salts 12, 13, 24, 29, 38, 39
sodium carbonate 39, 43, 60
stalactites and stalagmites 37
strontium 7, 8, 10, 15, 19, 46-9, 58, 60

toothpastes 10, 47

vacuum tubes 33, 51

water 14, 15

X-rays 11, 22, 47, 52-3